Twelve Friends

TWELVE FRIENDS
A Counting Book about Jesus' Disciples

First North American edition published 1991 by Augsburg, Minneapolis
First published 1991 by Scripture Union, London, England
Copyright © 1991 Joy Hutchinson

ISBN 0-8066-2559-7   LCCN 91-71037

Manufactured in the United Kingdom   AF 9-2559

95   94   93   92   91   1   2   3   4   5   6   7   8   9   10

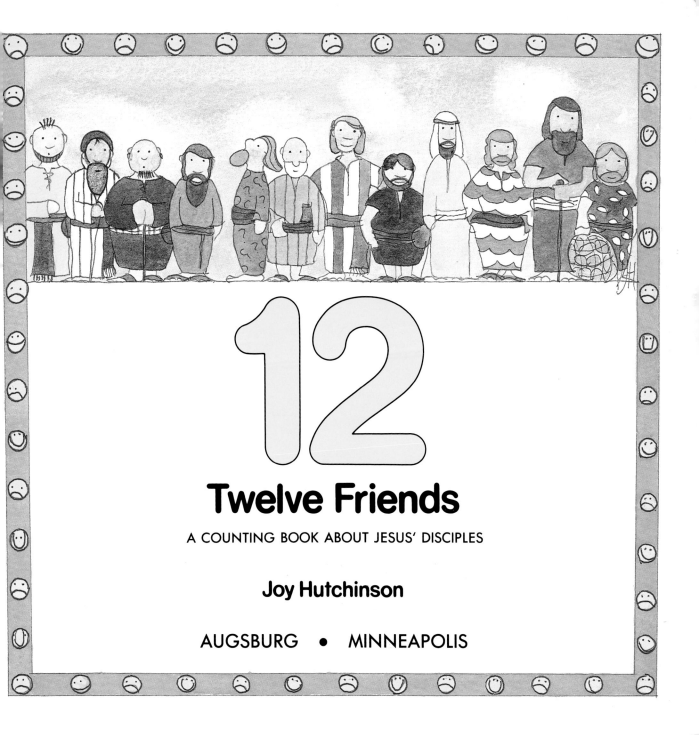

12

Twelve Friends

A COUNTING BOOK ABOUT JESUS' DISCIPLES

Joy Hutchinson

AUGSBURG • MINNEAPOLIS

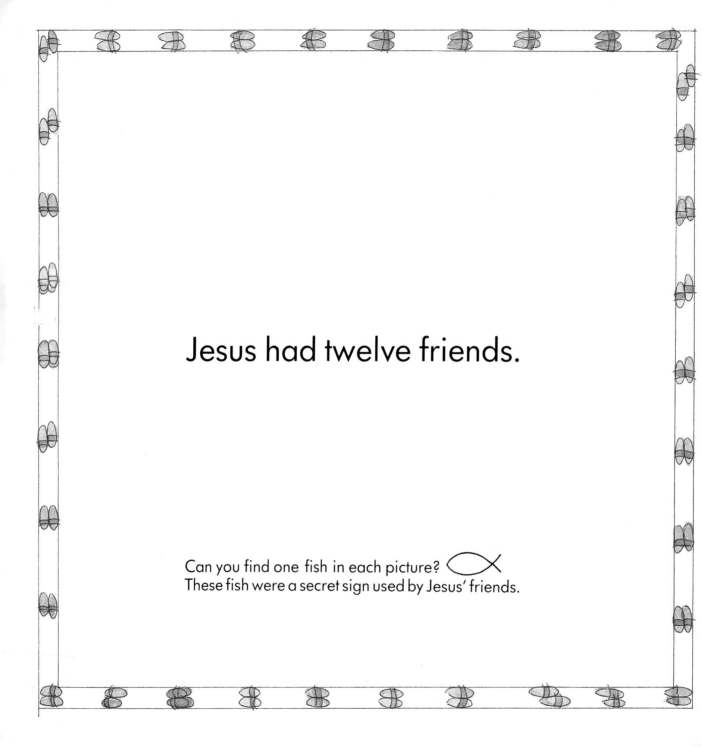

Jesus had twelve friends.

Can you find one fish in each picture?
These fish were a secret sign used by Jesus' friends.

One was Andrew.
He was a fisherman in Galilee.

Two was Peter,
Andrew's big brother.

Three was James.
He was mending his
nets when he met Jesus.

Four was John. He was Jesus' special friend.

Five was Philip. He lived near Andrew.

Six was Nathanael.
Philip told him about
Jesus.

Seven was Matthew.
He was a tax collector.

Eight was Thomas.
He was never sure
about things.

Nine was James.
He liked to keep cool.

Ten was Judas Iscariot. He loved money and in the end was not Jesus' true friend.

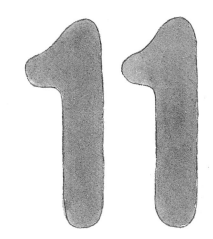

Eleven was another Judas. He liked to walk in the hills.

Twelve was Simon.
He was a thinker.

Jesus knew friends were important. He would like to be *your* friend, too.